The Traveler
A Journey through Life

DAN M. KHANNA

Copyright © 2014 Dan M. Khanna

All rights reserved.

ISBN: 0692326197
ISBN-13: 978-0692326190

DEDICATION

To My Mother

Who started my journey
Put me on a boat
To travel across oceans
With love, dignity and wisdom.

*"Two roads diverged in a wood, and I -
I took the one less traveled by,
And that has made all the difference."*

Robert Frost

CONTENTS

Prologue - In Retrospect

A Personal Note

The Traveler: A Passage Through Life	1
Death	8
What Little I Know	9
A Heart is a Lonely Hunter	10
Love is a Dream	11
A Life of Defeat	12
Yes, I Love You-	13
The Shattering of Dreams	14
How to Mend a Broken Heart	15
Love is a Curse	16
Eye of the Storm	17
In Search of Man	18
The Pendulum Swings	19
Love is a Razor's Edge	20
The World I Live In	21
Life is Like Weather	22
Friends! Where are They?	23
I am a Wonder	24
God, Almighty God	25
For We Were One	26
The Prophet of Doom	28
The Morning	30
The Winter of Discontent	31
Man Without Love	32
People	33
What Do I Write?	34
When Will I Ever Learn?	35
Love	36
Contentment	37
I Remember You	38
On Writing	39

I Am Not From This World	41
A Man Not of This World	42
Life of a Wanderer	44
The Evil Within Me	46
The Phoenix in You	47
My Relationship with Life	52
The End of End	54
What a Fitting Ending	55
The Cage of Life	56
Sky and the Sea	57
Life in a Bar	58
The End of Life	59
I Think I Live	60
I Think of My Life	61
The Mark of Life	63
The Path of Destiny	65
A New Life	67
The Twilight Zone	68
Happiness	69
Daughter	70
A Reflection	71
The River and the Ocean	73
The Decadence of Life	75
The Meat Market	78
The Empty Glass	80
A New Beginning	82
God's Favorite Person	83
Dreams	85
Standing on the Cliff	86
The Crossroads	88
The Razor's Edge	89
About My Life	90
The Story of Life	91
The Roller Coaster	93
The Storm	94
My Father, My Daughter	96

PROLOGUE

IN RETROSPECT

I am not a poet. I never intended to be a poet. It just happened, by chance, just like many things in my life. I read poetry as a young boy - Browning, Tennyson, Milton, and the other English poets. As I grew, I read the classics: Homer, Dante and others, not necessarily understanding all of them, but I enjoyed them anyway. Later, I relished the works of Khalil Gibran, Omar Khayyam and Rumi. I fell in love with Urdu poetry and absorbed the works of Mirza Ghalib and other Urdu poets. In essence, I read poetry regardless of the source.

It was 1983, when I wrote my first poem. It was a very challenging period for me. I was successful professionally, but I wanted to discover myself. I reflected on my life's journey and wondered where it will take me next. I saw myself as a traveler through life, visiting strange lands, meeting new people, and learning from new cultures and societies.

One day, I picked up a pen and started writing. I named the writing, "The Traveler". I did not know that it will become a poem.

I kept writing whatever came into my mind until I finished the poem. I did not know what I had written, but it felt good. I read my poem for the first time and liked it. I was writing for myself. It dawned on me that maybe I can write other poems. Initially, I wrote poems sporadically, but now I write frequently on whatever topic comes to mind.

I now have written hundreds of poems and will continue to write as long as I live. I never intended to be a poet, but I enjoy writing for myself. It makes me feel me. I am in touch with myself. It is a meditative stage. It is euphoric.

My travels continue.

Dan Khanna

A PERSONAL NOTE

"The Traveler" is my first poem, which I wrote in California in the early 1980's. I did not know I could write poetry. I knew I loved reading poetry. I don't know why I wrote it. Maybe I was trying to find some meaning in my life having traveled many distances. It just happened. After I wrote it, I felt good. Then, I started writing poetry more frequently and I have written over twelve hundred poems since writing "The Traveler".

I get ideas for poems as I write my journal or as I observe life around me. I create a title that later becomes a theme for a poem. Sometime later, I complete the poem. My muse comes in a crowded place where I can observe people. I carry my writing book and a fountain pen. All my poems are handwritten with pen and ink, a flow from my mind through the ink and onto the paper. Once I start a poem, I complete it in one writing spell. Later, as the collections of poems increase, I transfer them onto my computer under a book title. Such is my creative life in this worldly jungle.

The first book, The Traveler, contains sixty-seven poems written in chronological order as I reflected on many aspects of life and living, and what life tells us. It is continuous learning experience.

More coming,

Dan Khanna

September 12, 2014

THE TRAVELER

A PASSAGE THROUGH LIFE

As I traveled through the woods,
Searching for myself,
I came upon an old man
In a small hut.

He was pleased and surprised
To see a stranger
So far in the wilderness,
So far away from home.

He was alone but peaceful.

I was just alone.

He welcomed my intrusion
And pleasantly asked,
"Where do you go?"

"I don't know", I answered.

"Are you lost, my son?" he gently inquired.

"One is lost if one has a destination,
And cannot find the path
To reach it.

But I have no destination
I wander randomly
To unknown places and
To never ending hopes,

So, how can I be lost?"

His deep dark eyes gazed through me,
And felt the tempest in my mind.
He reached out his warm wrinkled hand.
And he pulled me down to his side.

"What bothers you, my son?"

"Life", I answered.

"Why does life bother you?" he asked.

I answered,
"For I do not know why I came into this world
For I do not know where I go from this world
For I do not know when I go from this world
And I know not what I am to do here."

He looked at me with tenderness,
And gently inquired,
"Why do you need to know all that?
Isn't it enough to know
That morning comes with the sun,
That flowers bloom in the spring,
That rivers run to the ocean,
That rain comes from the clouds?"

"Why know the mystery of life,
For in its mystery lies its beauty,
And, in its silence, solace."

I looked at him with arrogance.
His peace was war to me.
In defiance, I said,
"Is it sinful to ask:
Why the sun rises?
Why flowers bloom?
Why rivers rush to the seas?
Why rain comes?"

"This entire scheme of things
Has its beauty, horror and mystery.

I have seen the beauty
And basked in its joy.
I have seen its horror
And cried with sorrow.
Now I search its mystery
And find no peace."

"Why with so much beauty around,
There is so much pain?
Why someone is happy and
Someone is not?
And, why do I see sadness
In every joy?
Why does life and death
Exist side by side?"

"I seek life
For I am part of it;
Because I am part of it,
I need to understand my role,
So I can perform it,
To my best ability."

"Yes, my son," he politely spoke.
"You have a long way to go
Before you find the answer.
But, my friend," he warned,
"That answer
May allude you forever,
Or, that answer
May shatter your dreams,
Or, it may
Raise you to the levels of heaven,
Or, it may
Crush you through the depths of hell."

"As for myself,
I am content
With my travels through life.

My desires were simple,
And I asked for little."

His warm deep eyes
Searched through me,
His gentle wisdom
Calmed me.
I looked around to see
The calmness of the wilderness.
The freedom of the birds and flowers,
And how simple a life they lead.

"Yes, my learned friend," I sighed.
"Life is simple here,
But, tell me,
Why is this life simple and peaceful?"

The old man looked
At the flowers, and spoke,
"Look at the flowers,
How they bloom?
They suffer the harshness of nature,
Enjoy fair weather,
When spring comes, they bloom
When fall comes, they die.
And, sometimes,
They die with a storm."

"Their purpose is simple:
They have no desire
But to beautify the world.
They exist for a short time
And serve their purpose."

I sighed and answered,
"Alas, I could just see
The beauty of the flowers,
Which is immense and abundant,
But, I also see
The pain it goes through
In its short span of life."

"I see it survive with thorns
Ravaged by bees and insects
I see it fight with the weather,
Or be plucked at its prime
To please others."

"How it awaits its demise
With surrender and apprehension,
For it knows it is helpless,
And must die with the season."

"I live by the seasons of life,
What I was yesterday,
I am not today,
I will not be tomorrow.
And, when tomorrow ends,
I die like a flower,
And I will know not why."

The old man sighed
And held my hand,
"You complicate more
Than you unravel."

"See the ocean.
Its waves rhythmically carve the shores,
Its deep waters
Ascends to the clouds
And the winds carry them to the land,
Where it brings life
To plants and people."

I interrupted, and said,
"But what about the deepness of the ocean?

Who has fathomed it
And understood its mysteries?
Who has seen the darkness
That lurks in its bosom
Where light has never penetrated?

That same wind may
Bring life, peace and comfort,
May turn into storm
That may destroy
Ships, hopes and lives."

"Yes, my wise friend,
You chose to look at life
That makes you tranquil.

I chose to look at life
That makes me turbulent.

You accept the existence,
I question the beginning
And the end."

The old man looked at the sky and me
With shattering wisdom, he said,
"You seek an answer
That you may never find.
Nor find the peace
That you seek."

"You will remain
A traveler through life.

A life where you will
Never have a home.

You will live in inns and taverns,
None of which
Will be your own.

You will be a stranger to everyone,
Including yourself.

Your peace will come
At the end of your travels
If it ever ends;
For your travel may
Last through eternity."

I got up at these words
To bid him farewell.
I held his warm hand
And gently said,
"So be it.
Let me continue then
The quest I seek.
Maybe my purpose is to search
What I cannot find.
But in its search
I grow.
Your path in my travels,
Has enriched me
To search for peace and answers
That may reside in me.

I bid you farewell, my friend.
And you will always
Remain in my travels."

DEATH

Death
Thou I seek,
I see you through life.

I lived for you
Existed for you
And, sought your solace
In the turbulence of times.

You were the goal,
Living was attainment.

It is a pity,
That to achieve
The tranquility of your comfort
I lived an agony of life.

A moment of eternal peace,
For a lifetime of sorrow.

WHAT LITTLE I KNOW

I write of Life
As if I know it all.

Yet, each day of living
Tells me what little I know.

I came, I lived, I died:
It all seemed like a dream.

I don't remember,
How I lived.

I don't remember,
Why I died.

It all happened so fast.

I was just getting used to Life,
When God said, "It is over."

Over, for I was mediocre,
That even I didn't know.

I couldn't even remember,
Anything I had accomplished.

What I did in Life,
Was just an existence.

And, I went through Life,
Never realizing,
What little I knew.

A HEART IS A LONELY HUNTER

A heart is a lonely hunter.
It searches for love,
Hoping to capture it,
And, proudly showing it to
Friends and foes,

Yet in that search,
It faces danger,
Surprise and shock.

But, like a hunter,
It seeks its prey.

One day
The hunter becomes the hunted.

For it may die
At the hand of love.
And, the lonely hunter
Is no more.

LOVE IS A DREAM

Love is dream
That breaks when we wake.
Sometimes we remember
Sometimes we don't.

We may be in love,
Yet not know.
We may dream.
We are in love
Or is a fantasy
Or a painful experience.

Maybe, love should remain a dream,
For in dreams there is hope,
If love is beautiful,
But, dreams are unreal,
If love hurts.

Sometimes illusion is better than reality,
And, reality is sometimes an illusion.
An illusion, that we live in,
An illusion, that we die in,
For love is just a dream.
And, maybe remains a dream.

A LIFE OF DEFEAT

A life of defeat is hard to take,
Especially if the defeat
Was caused by oneself.

How does one tell oneself,
That you are a failure,
And, that you caused it all.
Failure and defeat in all,
All that is human,
And, all that is life.

Defeat in love,
Leaves pain and hurt.
Failure of friends,
Leaves silence and suffering.
Pain of living,
Makes survival a struggle.
Loss of faith,
Leaves despair and depression,
And to lose oneself
Is the end of life.

How to prolong life,
When it has ended.

YES, I LOVE YOU

Yes, I love you!
The words I have spoken
To you many times,
Sometimes knowingly
Sometimes unknowingly
But, every time
I meant it.

Love is such a strong force
That creates emotions
We didn't know we had
Some good, some bad.
Some we control,
Some we don't.

Love brings us together
Pulls us apart
For that is love
A part of life
That cannot change.
Yes, I love you.

THE SHATTERING OF DREAMS

We all have dreams
To dream of beautiful things,
and life.
To dream of happiness
and contentment.
To dream of peace
and tranquility.
To dream of opportunity
and challenge.

We dream all our life
Hoping to realize our dreams
During one lifetime.
Yet, we see those dreams
Shattering like glass.

Dreams are like glass.
We can see through it,
Yet it is there before us.
We can touch it
But can't see it.
We admire its beauty
But can never be in it.
It is smooth, but
When cut, sharp.
One moment it is a piece of art
In another moment a jagged edge.
It can preserve and kill.
We want it,
Yet we are afraid of it.
It is like a glass.
A glass that breaks easily
Just like the shattering of dreams.

HOW TO MEND A BROKEN HEART

How to mend a broken heart
When it is torn beyond repair.
No amount of time
Can heal the wound.
No amount of tears
Can seal the cut.
The cut is deep
And scars forever.
A symbol of love
Forever carved in your soul
A mark
That identifies you
As a wounded soldier,
A soldier who fought for a cause.
But, that cause is no more,
Just a memory
That lingers in the mind
With flashes and remembrances
Of time lost forever
Yet staying within
And inside
And lasting through eternity
As I begin
To pick the pieces
The pieces of heart.
I will never be able
To find them all.

LOVE IS A CURSE

Love is a curse
That must befall
All those who love.
For love
Will tear them apart
Or, give them happiness
For a while,
But never,
For a lifetime.

Blessed be those
That have love
For a lifetime.
For they should cherish it
As a gift from God.

But for those
For whom love is a dream,
Life is a curse.

For to feel love
Is a curse
And for not to love
Is even a bigger curse
It is better to be alone
Than to be
Lonely without love.

It is a curse to feel love
For love is a curse.

EYE OF THE STORM

The storm awaits me
It needs a feast, a body
That it can toss up and down
And delight in the jolts of life
While I ride the crest
And crash to the sea
Waiting for another wave
To hurl me
In all directions.

I go in all directions
But remain at the same place
Waiting for the eye of the storm
To bring a moment of calm
Through which I can see the sky
Clear and far
Waiting for the storm to hit
So I can continue the struggle
And enjoy a moment of peace
In the eye of the storm.

IN SEARCH OF MAN

Where is man?
It is not the many faces
That walks gloomily in the street.

Where is man?
It is not that exists and survives
In the tyranny of the few.

Where is man?
It is not that exists passively
To let others do his thinking.

Where is man?
That was supposed to think
And create a world of joy and happiness.

Where is man?
It is not the same person
That rapes the place it lives in.

Where is man?
It is not the same person
That differentiates, rebukes and kills.

Where is man?
That was supposed to
Create a heaven on earth.

We live around men,
But, there are no men.
We still
Search for man.

THE PENDULUM SWINGS

The pendulum swings
Between life and death
And at each end
It pauses
To decide where to go.

But, does it really decide?
Or, is it forced to decide?
Or, the decision is made already
By the forces of the universe?

For it swings again
Not knowing when to stop
For it, the stop
Means the end of life
The end of its rhythm
But not its purpose
Which is to swing
Between life and death.

It swings
Because of nature.
It reverses
Because of nature.
Why it does that
Only nature knows.

But it swings
In perpetual motion
To the rhythm of life
Or to the rhythm of death
For eventually
They are the same.

The pendulum swings
To keep alive
And to let nature
Decide when it should stop.

LOVE IS A RAZOR'S EDGE

Love is a razor's edge

A sharp line
that divides
hurt from happiness.

Walking that line
is itself painful.

Yet from that pain
may come some pleasure.

Pain and pleasure
do exist
side by side
Each having
its own joy

Just like love
on the razor's edge.

THE WORLD I LIVE IN

The world I live in
Seems ancient and alien.

The life that I live
Seems struggle and survival.

The people that I live with
Seem callous and cruel.

The friends that I live with
Seem indifferent and indignant.

The relatives that I deal with
Seem dangerous and demanding.

The lovers that I live with
Seem separate and selfish.

The children I live with
Seem carefree and careless.

The God that I worship
Seems ignorant and impotent.

I will soon pass from this world
The world that I live in

But the world will go on
And on, and on, and on.

LIFE IS LIKE WEATHER

Life
is like weather.
Sometimes hot,
sometimes cold,
sometimes warm,
sometimes cool.

Changes in season
are painful yet pretty
And continuous
just like life.
Each different scenery
some beautiful
some not.

The rhythm
of the seasons
As life passes
through different worlds
each with its own colors
and flavors
each with its own beauty
and its own time span.
Eventually
ravaged by the next season.

Life, like the weather,
Goes on forever.

FRIENDS! WHERE ARE THEY?

I hope
that after my death
I don't have any friends.

For in this life
Friends have just hurt.

They gloat
on your failures.
Delight
in your suffering.
Envy
your joy.
Stab you
in your back.
Compliment
when they don't mean it.
Sympathize
with joy.

In time
As it does happen
You lose your friends.
We become alone
As we
were destined to be.

Friends are rare
If you find one.
Friends!
Where are you?

I AM A WONDER

The wonders of life
are many.

I am
one of the wonders
of life.

But, remember
Not all wonders
are discovered.

Some will lie dormant
or, will just fade away
without anyone knowing.

There are many
such wonders
Like me.

GOD, ALMIGHTY GOD

God
The Almighty God

What we have made of Him

The Terror of the Universe
The Fear of Mankind.

We spend money
To pray to Him
To keep His wrath
away from us

To cover our sins
To seek salvation

As we continue to grow
Immoral and sinners

We learn not from Him
For He is the one
Called Love.

FOR WE WERE ONE

For each day
I was with you
I said to myself
I never want to apart from you

You and I were one.

One and only ones that mattered
The rest was just life
As we passed it
Or, it passed us

But, we didn't care
For we were one.

We joked and laughed
We cried
And we were there
In each other's arms
To hold and to console

Even when we were angry
We felt tenderness
For we were one.

Then came a storm
That swept into our lives
A storm of discontent
That uprooted our hopes
And shattered our dreams

We wanted to be one
But the storm pushed us away.

We reached out
But could not hold

And we plunged
Into an abyss
And then we were gone

Gone together in a different world.
For we were one
And will always remain one.

THE PROPHET OF DOOM

As I see
the world around me,
I feel it collapsing
Inward...shrinking
Pulling
everything around it
Making everything insignificant.

Soon I see
the oceans evaporate,
The mountains
become valleys,
The rivers creeks,
And people ants.

But, it doesn't stop.
It goes on.

Soon the mass shrinks
further and further,
Finding holes within holes,
Each layer
disappearing into another.

Soon what was left
Just a ball
with markings on it.
Lines and dots
The remains of civilization
That was once there.

Soon the ball shrinks
Into a dot.
A point.
And then
it is no more.

One could see clearly
Through the open sky,
Where once was a world
Was now a clear vision
A vision of unknown
And a vision of everything.

THE MORNING

The morning
Full of surprises,
What will the day bring?
How many dreams
will get shattered?
What revelations will I have?

Will the day be eventful?
Will it be an ordinary day?

Or, will it be a day
When I won't even know
That I have lived through the day.

Will I feel happy when the day ends?
Happy that I did something worthwhile,
Or, happy that it is over?

To go to sleep,
To wait for the next morning.

Yes, morning
The best time of the day
When you still have hopes
and dreams
Of a great day.

THE WINTER OF DISCONTENT

The winter chill passes through me
Shaking my bones
and emotions,
Making them cold, and
Wishing for warmth
of different sorts.

A blanket to keep the body warm,
A body to keep the body warm.
One is real, the other is unreal.

Reality is but a moment,
For just a fleeting second
When unreal is real.

We live unreal lives,
searching for reality
That keeps passing by
Like the winter chill.

The body searching for warmth
That it will never find
For chill is the reality.

MAN WITHOUT LOVE

A man without love
Is like a tree without leaves.

It cannot hear
the sound of winds
rustling through the leaves,
The joy of seeing
the leaf growing,
the pain of the leaf falling,
the richness of its color
the smell of its existence.

The tree is barren
Without a natural covering
Of warmth and beauty
with no admirers
and ready to exist
in nature's path.

It is a lonely sight
Extending its branches
to invite wilderness
to invite death
For death will end
its ugly existence
Just like - - man
A man without love.

PEOPLE

People, yes people
We got to live with people
And get hurt by them.

People - - with some many complexes
Different, yet the same.
Same, for the overall goal
Is to survive.
Different, for we go about it
In different ways
And we don't understand how,
We look at things one way
And interpret it the other.
The other remains a mystery
Which we try to unravel
In our own way.

People confound us
for people are different.
We are different.
I am different.
Through times and seasons
Through land and mountains
Through age
We constantly change,
People change
And we have to live with them
With people.

WHAT DO I WRITE?

What do I write
When there is so much to write?
Thoughts come in fleeting glances
Before I can pen them down
They escape me
While I grasp at remnants.

So much to write
As I look around
Mostly sad, mostly unworthy
Writing about human survival
In which we are failing
And upsetting people
Who do not want to know
That they are making it fail
for it is always the other person.

What do I write
When life offers so little?
To write that is good
Except some glorifying
Events of a single person
When our system
That created us
Fails before us
And we do not know
Whether to write about it
Or prevent it from falling.
It will fall one day
And I will write about it
But then there will
Be no one to read it.

WHEN WILL I EVER LEARN?

When will I ever learn?
Learn that what I want
is not what I'll get,
And what I get, hurts.
Always hurts
and this goes on.

I learn to unlearn
Unlearn what I should have not learnt
Unlearn what life is all about.

A place for people,
who use people,
To become
What they cannot achieve.

It is a world of users.
People who use people
To be people
But not the people
they should be.

I am in that world.

Where people don't count
Except when it helps.
But, life goes on,
And I live with people
who are not real people
But people who live a life
that has no meaning.

I am part of that.

Life without meaning,
Can I change?
Can I unlearn what I have learnt?
Only time will tell.

LOVE

Love, is just a word
It conveys
joy and sadness.
The pain it causes
The suffering it brings
The agony it creates.

But, we still want love.
For its pangs make us live
Feel like humans.

The feeling we want
But cannot stand
The love that we want
Does not exist.

It exits in our dreams,
our fantasy
An idealistic world
Where all is true
But nothing is true.

We live two lives,
Dreams and reality,
And they are far apart
And, love does it all.

CONTENTMENT

I feel contented
Now that I am in love.
Love with someone
That enlivens you
That brings life to you,
Knowing that life
Is just a memory of today.

Today determines the future
The future, that is unknown
We are there, yet not there,
Each second moves us in the future
Leaving the past behind.

Past that was not a past
Past that I am not proud of
But, the future opens me,
scares me, yet
Future is where I must live
For future is where my life is
In future lies my happiness
And, in future, lies my salvation.

The past came and went
Future is where I belong.
The love opens the future
A place where I bloom
And find contentment.

It is my life
Love is my life
And in love
I find life
And contentment.

I REMEMBER YOU

I remember you,
    When you are not there.
I remember you,
    When I feel your presence.
I remember you,
    When your thoughts touch mine.
I remember you,
    When I feel your eyes gaze into me.
I remember you,
    When I feel your tenderness.
I remember you,
    When I feel your embrace.
I remember you,
    When I think of your world.
I remember you,
    When I want to share happiness.
I remember you,
    When I want to share my pain.
I remember you,
    When there is no one there for me.
I remember you,
    When life just wants you.
I remember you,
    When the world is just you.

That is,
I remember you,
    All the time.

ON WRITING

Why write?

It unburdens the soul
It puts on paper
What I feel.

My thoughts,
my emotions,
my feelings.

It is an effort
To communicate to the world
About me
So I may be understood
By the world
That I don't understand.

But writers write
To enrich the world
Or to enrich themselves.

The writer is a dreamer.
Dreams have many facets.
Dreams can be pleasant.
Dreams can be scary.

The writer shares dreams
With the world.

Is the world affected?
Maybe yes, maybe no,
But the writer is.

The writer is transformed
By each writing.
Each writing
opens hidden doors.
Each writing
unleashes passions.
Each writing
makes you learn about yourself.
Each writing
enriches the soul.

Writing is a growth experience
A part of life
That wants to grow.

Each writing
is a living experience.
An experience
that is always changing.

For as life and world change
So should mind and soul.

Writing is a change in life.
It is a life of sharing.
Sharing of dreams and fantasy
A sharing of hope, ideas and vision.

A writer shares
his life, his world
And sharing is noble
And writers share themselves.

I AM NOT FROM THIS WORLD

It is true
I did not want to be born,
And, yet, I did
Something or someone
that controls my life,
decided it for me
without letting me know
That I will be born
Even though
I did not want
to be born.

Now I endure life,
Which I did not want,
And question
where I came from,
but definitely,
not from this world.

For this world is crazy,
Craziness that makes
the world
spin around and around
looking for itself.

I count not have been from here
Where I come from
Only God knows.

A MAN NOT OF THIS WORLD

There are times in life
When a man searches his soul
To question not his life
But, to question
His role in this world.

Do we belong in the world?
Is the world too ahead of us?
Or are we ahead of this world?

Many times we feel
out of rhythm
With the rest of the world.

Nostalgia does that,
Future does that.

Are we in the right place,
Why are we struggling
to remain in the present.

The past haunts us,
The future daunts us
And the present
remains an existence.

Am I a man of this world?

I don't know.
Sometimes, I am,
Sometimes, I am not.

Is anyone of this world?

That is a question,
no one can answer.

But, I know,
I am not
A man of this world.

LIFE OF A WANDERER

The life of a wanderer
Is a life of constant growth.
Learning new ways
In an ever changing world,
Knowing that wandering
Is always unsettling,
For you are
never in one place
for long.

For a wanderer,
Change is constant
and a wanderer
thrives on change.

But no place is home,
and to the wanderer
each place
is a home.
Temporary, it may be,
But it is home.

A home you feel and learn from,
But you are never part of that home,
For home is security
And a wanderer does not like security.

Security weakens the wanderer.
The wanderer's strength
comes from being alone.
A loner in the world,
where everyone is a loner
In one way or another.

For it is a wanderer
who explores the world
for those who remain the same.

For it is a wanderer
who makes the world grow
And in its growth gets killed,
That is the life of a wanderer.

THE EVIL WITHIN ME

What lurks inside me
That tells me
Life is not what I want.

What constantly pesters me
To question life
As if
life and I are separate
Existing without each other
As friends or foe.

What is inside me,
I don't know,
But, I feel it
Its presence in me
Guiding and advising
Through the journey of life.

At times it sounds evil
For I don't want to listen to it.
It speaks the truth,
But who wants the truth.
It criticizes me,
But who wants criticism.

My fantasies are my reality,
Reality itself is pain
And this evil causes pain
For it talks of reality,
For it talks of facing the truth,
Trust is not always right,
For it hurts the living.

And all this is caused
By the evil
That lurks inside us.
It stalks all of us,
It is the evil we need.

THE PHOENIX IN YOU

Sometimes we just lose
Lose what we have gained.
Losing, a valuable experience
Losing oneself is difficult
Wondering, when the losing will stop.

I was on top
Top of the world
Peak of my life
Peak of my career
Power and money
The brotherhood of corruption
False glory and
ego boosting.

An artificial world
that we dream to live in.
Not knowing
That reality is but a dream
For dreams always end
No matter how long you sleep.

It was a dream, that said
You are on top
A top with no bottom
A hollow
For when you fall
You fall fast
With no support
We just fall
and fall, and fall
Wondering who will hold us
Stop us
from falling further.

Our hands reach out
To grasp what we can,
But, air is difficult to grasp
Empty holds of vacuum
As one gets ready
To hit bottom
You want the bottom
You want the hit rather
Than an endless fall.

You stop breathing
Hoping to prolong your life
But, the fall continues.

Then, a miracle happens,
You feel the fall slowing
Unseen hands reach out
A cushion is born
You slow down
You stop falling.
The fall ends.

You are being held
By unknown hands.
What is that hand?

A hand of God?
A hand of life?
A hand of hope?
A hand of forgiveness?
A hand of humility?
A hand of vulnerability?
A hand of self-realization?

Self-realization that comes
When one is near an end.

At that time
All life flashes
in front of us.
Our sins
shine in bright colors,
The colors
blinding us
Darkening our minds.

We depend on the unseen hands
To hold us
in mid-air
Still helpless and unsure
But, a moment
To collect thoughts.

Am I safe?
Or just a delay of death.
Thoughts move in circles.
Where am I?
In the middle,
Or near the end.

Can I reach out
and touch the top
Or, am I too far in the abyss?

I cannot reach out.
There is no foothold.
A precarious moment
As I am being held.

Then, you call on yourself
Your inner strength
Your spiritual strength
To move up
Up to the top.

You hope.
You pray.
You have faith,
faith in yourself.
You move
The inner fuel of life
moves you.

You feel the movement
You are moving
Moving up
Slowly at first.

You pray.
You meditate.
Your heart is your engine.
Your faith is your driver.
Your mind, the fuel.

You move
faster and faster.
You are approaching the top
You touch the top.
Hold it.

You have gained
What you had lost.

The years of losses
Has given you strength.
To rise to the top.

The losses were the energy
That energized your future
And now you face the future
Wise from losses
Peace from hurt
And knowing

That an unknown force
Is behind you
To be there
When you need it most
It holds you like a baby
Giving warmth and comfort,
and love.
That hand
and that force
Is God
and if you believe that
It is in you.

MY RELATIONSHIP WITH LIFE

My relationship with life
is unique.
I live life,
but I am not a part of it.

Life embraced me at birth
to give health and security.

I resisted it,
For I did not want
to live by its rules,
For I belonged to another world.

I had my own rules,
so we clashed.
Sometimes I won,
sometimes life won.

My victories were small,
Life's victories were great.

Overall, I began losing,
But, still life could not eliminate me,
For I was me
and in me
was my own unique strength.

For life could destroy
everything around me,
It could not destroy
what was in me.

So we fought and argued,
But lived together,
For you are part of life
'Til you die.

And that is,
My relationship with life.

THE END OF END

The end of end,
What is it?

Is it a place
from where you go nowhere?
Or, is it that time
when time stops completely?
Is it that feeling,
that encompasses all feelings,
and there are no more feelings left?

Is there an end
where everything ends,
And life becomes still eternally?

Is there an end
to the future,
So one doesn't worry about it,
And we forever live in the present.

What is an end?
End is when all things cease,
Yet nothing ceases.

Does life end?
Or does it start a new beginning
for a new end?

Where does knowledge end?
So what is the end?

It would be nice to know
the end of end.

WHAT A FITTING ENDING

The end that must happen
It happens to all of us.

Young, old, good, bad
All have an end in common.

But, what is a fitting end?

Does each person deserve a unique end?
What is a unique end?
A turbulent end to a turbulent life?
A peaceful end to a peaceful life?
A troubled end to a troubled life?
A happy end to a happy life?

In the end, the end is peaceful.

Even troubled souls
Find a peaceful end.

But, in the end
it doesn't matter.

No matter what life one lives,
The end discriminates no more,
End is common to all
And peaceful to all.

It is the only befitting end
To all forms of life
For all ways of living,
In the end,
it is just an end,
A fitting end to everything,
And that,
is a fitting end.

THE CAGE OF LIFE

Is it me or life
I don't know,
But the cage of life
That envelops me
From life to death
Is shrinking.

Shrinking,
because I am growing big,
Or, life is shrinking.

Is it my growing expectations
of life,
Or, is it the decaying of life
By life itself.

I am in a cage of life
I can see it
But cannot touch it.

Life cannot release me
From its cage.
For life is meant to envelop
And keep you in the cage,
And keep you there.

Yet, one wants freedom,
Freedom from the cage,
Freedom from the life
That keeps me in the cage.
And keeps you there.

I want freedom from life.
I want out of the cage.

SKY AND THE SEA

There is a place
Where the sky meets the sea.

It is a place I can see
But not reach.
As I travel towards it,
The further it moves.

It is always there
Yet not there,
A place
Where there is oneness,
Yet a place not reachable.

I can see it,
Eyes don't lie.

Yet eyes do lie
For they see an image
And believe
that image is reality.

But, reality is just an image.

An image that one sees,
But never grasps.

It remains an illusion
And a dream
And a hope
Just like the place
Where the sky meets the sea.

LIFE IN A BAR

I sit in a bar
Observing people I do not know.
Talking to people I do not know.
Yet I feel content.

People listen.
People talk.
Learning from people
Whom I do not know.

For a few hours
This place is home.
A peaceful home
Where I am what I am.
No pretentiousness
No pressures
Just a place to be me
To share my thoughts and feelings
And not be evaluated
And not be judged.

Someone to listen.
Someone to talk.
A friendly place
Where everyone is someone
Searching for only one thing
A home away from home
A place to be oneself
A place where one is free.

THE END OF LIFE

The end of life
Seems so bewitching
Crossing threshold
From living to eternity
Though eternity is unknown
It is tempting
Tempting to the lonely soul
That sees alone around
Alone in a world
That itself is so lonely.
Alone in a world
That seeks mediocrity
But like grows
Leaving behind
What doesn't grow
Just life me
Who refuses to grow.
To grow to what?
A world falling apart
A world killing itself
To grow toward death is natural
To grow prematurely to death
Is unnatural.
But what is natural and unnatural,
It is a fine line
What is natural
May seem unnatural.
What is unnatural,
May seem natural.
The whole of life
Is a pendulum
From reality to dream
That comes to an end
With the end of life,
But does it?

I THINK I LIVE

I think, I live.
Why? I don't know.
I don't want to.
Why should I?
What has life given me?
Life that was not my choosing.
I can make what I want of life.
But, can a child in an African refugee camp?
Can a child in an Indian village?
What is life for that child?
Surviving by taking care of the parents.
Parents who procreated
Called it a gift of God,
So that they can exist
While their children work
To take care of parents.
Yet they live
Not knowing what life is all about
Except to feed parents,
For their parents
Gave them life.
The gift of life
Which we must all cherish,
But not question
What that life is.
For questioning is not living
Living is existence
Existence by rules of others
For which I must survive
But then I may live
Or think I live
For that life is not mine.

I THINK OF MY LIFE

When I think of my life,
I am surprised to learn
That I have lasted so long.

The mistakes I made,
The follies I committed,
Should have sent me
To the grave
Way before my time.

But, then I was protected
How, by whom or why,
I don't know.

As I continue to learn
about me
I uncover
So much I don't know about me.

Each layer
Reveals a new one,
Some frightening,
Some intriguing,
Some challenging.

But me - all me
Each layer existing in life
With its own message
Each layer
Creating its own world
A world that drifts away from me
Yet is part of me.

I exist to maintain an equilibrium
Between two drifting worlds.

I am in the middle
Balancing life
That wants to hold me.
I hold on
Learning at each stage
with each learning
I think of my life
A life that teaches me every day.

THE MARK OF LIFE

The mark of life
Is what you make of it.

But what you make of it,
Only you know.

For life eludes you,
You can search for it,
You may feel you have it,
You may feel you control it,
Then it slips.

Life cannot be cornered
or controlled.
It ignores you.
It directs you.

You are at its mercy.
It determines your course
even if you think
it is your course.

Do you control life?
Or life controls you?
That is an eternal question,
Which no one has
ever answered correctly.

Life is life
and you are just part of it.

You will never be life
and life will never fully embrace you,
For it wants to retain its mystery,
And you are the mystery.

You are part of life
life includes you,
But you are never life
and life never you.

You are just
the mark of life.

THE PATH OF DESTINY

There are so many roads in life
Some are easy to travel,
Some are hard.
Some straight,
Some curved.
Some plain,
Some beautiful.
Some dull,
Some scary.
Some even,
Some undulating.

All roads
Eventually lead
To just an end.
And that is your end
The end as you describe
The end as you feel.

Is it a goal?
Is it a purpose?

Who determines
Which road to take?
You, or someone else?

You travel,
So maybe you.

But is it you?
Or, someone with you?
Or, without you?

Why are some paths a struggle,
Some easy?

Is the path your destiny?
You direct the path,
Or does the path direct you?

It is for you to know
The difference,
For it is your destiny
And your path.

A NEW LIFE

What is a new life?

Does it start the day
You are born?
Or, does it start
When we realize
That our life has just begun?
Or, does it start
When we realize
It is not what we thought
What it really was?
Or, does it start
Having lived part of it
That we realize
That it is not
What we meant?
Or, does it start
when we realize
That we have lived it
Without ever living it,
And now it is the end
And we can't do too much?
Or, does it start
When we die
having learnt the lesson of life?

We realize
Life is not how we lived,
So, it just ends
For a time
And we start
A new life.

Is there a right time
To start a new life
For the past is no more
Only an unknown
That is a new life.

THE TWILIGHT ZONE

The twilight of life
Has diminishing hopes
After a long existence.

The final sunset
Which has its best view,
For it is the last
That the eyes will see.

As the sun sinks,
So does life
Which the sun will never see again
For there is no sunrise.

A night of reflection
A night of remembrance
Of the first sunrise
Which was so beautiful.

But as the day wore on
The sun scorched life
Leaving memories
And a beautiful sunset of hopes
And dreams.

As I bid farewell
To the final sunset
The night approached
The final night
From which there is no sunrise.

It is the night of nights
The final end
The end of all ends
The twilight of life.

HAPPINESS

There is an art to happiness
That I have not mastered
I keep missing it
By wide margins.

Many times
I can't even find it.
I don't even know
When I lose it
Where I misplace it
And then it is gone.

Gone for a long stretch of time
In which I forget
What happiness was all about
I lose touch with it
I forget it
I can't even seem to recognize it
Even if it stands in front of me
Face to face.

I see the face of an alien
I don't know
We pass each other
Without recognition
And go our ways
Maybe never to cross paths again
But remain strangers
Forever.
For it is one art
That I will never master.

DAUGHTER

A daughter is a delight
Especially if you have
The one I have.

She brightens me
My life and my world
She makes me feel
A complete person
A man who loves.

She is hope.
She is future.

A new world
That will brighten
With her presence.

A life
That will be rich
With her in it.

A world
That will rejoice
With her presence.

And, that is my daughter
A person of the future
And a gift to the world.

She is mine
Will remain mine
For she is my daughter
A daughter of the world
And a delight to the world.

A REFLECTION

A reflection
On life
Portrays an image
That is scary and unknown.

Where have I been?
What was I?
Where am I?
What am I?
Questions, questions, questions...
Seeking an answer
In the reflection
Of my soul.

A reflection
That is distorted
Life the ripples in the water
Or, a curvature in the mirror
You can see,
But not see.
It is there
But, not there.

You reach for it
But it remains an illusion.
You touch it
And it is not there.

A reflection
Is just a memory
Of life as we have lived
As life we have known
As we have experienced.

A reflection
It is me, it is us
It is within me
It is within us
It is what I am
It is me.

THE RIVER AND THE OCEAN

The place
The union
Of the river
And the ocean
Where two different
Worlds meet.
One to swallow,
One to be swallowed.
One ending its journey,
The other starting.
One following a course,
The other creating a course.
One disappearing into depths,
Other concealing its depths.

The river
A passage through land
Of lives and people
Of different worlds
With different hopes
Of different existence.

The ocean
Creating its own existence
Of vastness and deepness
Pounding on the shores
To make a mark
On the world
Accountable to only itself
With its own deepness
And its own darkness.

A study of contrast
Of equal and unequal,
Both bodies of water
Yet so different,
One having a beginning
And an end.

The other,
Just a vast space,
With continued existence,
Determining its own
Beginning and end.

The union
Of two unequals
Is a sight
Where calmness
And turbulence
Clash.
Like life
At its end
Is swallowed
By death,
Just life a
River
Immersing
Into the
Ocean.

THE DECADENCE OF LIFE

The empty faces
With expectant desires
The selling of a body
For money
The violation of the body
For pleasure
In the decay of mankind
The decadence of life.

Look at the streets
Unkempt and unclean
Just like the soul
That needs cleansing.
But why clean
When enough filth
Exists to go around
For buyers and sellers.

In a greedy world
Everything is for sale
As long as the buyers exist.

Women sell, girls sell,
Young and old,
Mothers and daughters,
Virgins and seasoned,
Sell what they have
A gift of God
To bidders....
Men.

Men who buy
For pleasure
For ego
For gratification
For power
For esteem
For manliness.

To conquer
That womb
That brought them
In this world,
That passage
That opened the world
Of life
For them to live and breathe.

To punish
The mother
That endured them
In her womb
And nourished them
To cultivate
A new life.

But man
Must inject
His helplessness
Into the womb
Of life
To show
That he is finally free
Of all the ancient bonds
That bind
Life to birth
For it is his birthright
To free himself
From the womb of tranquility
To a world of violation
Of life
Because in a man's world
He controls
The womb.

The womb
That generates life
For it is his life
That he now controls
For what he controls
Is decadence of life.

THE MEAT MARKET

The hungry eyes
The leering faces
The gyrating bodies
Slithering in desire
For another body
To overcome the loneliness
That comes from life
And its pressures.

It is the night
To not be alone
But with someone
Just for the night
For night is long
And desire is strong.

Tomorrow,
Yes, tomorrow,
It will be over
With regret
After a passion
That had to be filled.

The women
All dressed up
Writhing in sensuous movements
Attracting the attention
Of wanton men
Whose only desire
Is to score....
Get a woman.

It is a night
To woo
And release
The pent up frustration
Of life.

Tonight is the night
When bodies mingle
To share loneliness
To be desired.
To be wanted
Just for the night
For who knows
What may come tomorrow.
Live for the night
For a new day
May usher the reality
Of the last night.

It may have been a dream
A moment of pleasure
For rejuvenating
The mind and the ego
To feel alive.

I made it
I got it
An empty gift.

THE EMPTY GLASS

The empty glass
In an empty bar
Is a place of hope
Is a place of faith.

It is near the end
Approaching closing time
The lights are dimming
And losing their luster.

The night is long
And lonely.

It is the end
Of a long day
Which started with hope
And ended in despair.

It is cold.
It is quiet.
All have gone
But I wait.

Wait for hope
For a last drink
Only if someone would pour
And fill my glass.

Even half a glass.

I look.
I stare
At the empty glass.

I want the glass
In front of me
To see
To touch
To feel
To imagine.

All that is hope
All that is faith.

It will come.
It will pour.
My glass will fill.
The people will come.
I will not be alone.
I will drink.
I will enjoy.
It will be great.
It will be life.

A life
That is mine.
A life
That is full.
Like the glass
In front of me.

But then I wake up
From my dream
Of hope and faith
To see the reality
Of the empty bar
At the closing time
In the middle of the night
Before the dawn
To stare
At what's before me
A glass
Just an empty glass.

A NEW BEGINNING

The skin sheds
Leaving a carcass
that is alive
and ready for change.

A new skin
grows
to envelope
the carcass
to give it
a new color
a new texture.

It is a new beginning
of a new life.

GOD'S FAVORITE PERSON

God does have favorites.
He does like some more than others.
Why? We don't know.

I am God's favorite.
He likes me more than others.
He watches me constantly.
He has time for me.
How do I know?

Let me tell you.

Look at all the challenges
That He throws at me!
Look at the barriers
That He puts in my path!
Look at the pain of living
That He creates for me!
Look at the hurt
That He bestows on me.

Well, maybe
He doesn't do all that
Maybe, I do it to myself.

But, I am His creation.
Why me?
Why do I need to keep
Rising from the ashes?

Because God likes me.
I am His chosen one.
He wants me to be the best
A seasoned human.

A human who has
Seen and experienced all
Good and bad
Pleasure and pain.

A person
Who has been guided by life
Towards perfection.

I strive
For perfection!
I think.

Only God knows
For I am his favorite person.

DREAMS

The dreams
Come and go
When you are asleep
When you are awake.

Dreams
Are part of life.

What are dreams?
What is reality?
Which is real?

Dreams are your hope
While reality is existence.
Which is what?
Do we know?

Do I exist?
I don't know.
Do I dream?
I don't know.

Am I a dream?
Am I an existence?
Am I real,
Or, just an illusion?

I touch me.
I don't feel.
I look
But, I cannot see.
I think,
But, I do not know.

What am I?
A person?
A reality?
Or, just a dream.

STANDING ON THE CLIFF

As I stand on the edge
At the precipice of life
I see the ocean below me
Hammering at the cliff.

The waves beckon me
With undulating rhythm.

I admire the beauty
Though dangerous it is.
Beauty can be dangerous.
I like the scene
But am afraid of its force.
To be with the waves
Is tempting
To get there
Is hazardous.

I am there
And not there.
I am at the edge
Looking below
At the sea
Trying to carve a hole
In the cliff.

The gust of wind
Shakes my thoughts
And carries me
Towards the waves.

Will I fall?
Will I soar?

Will it push me
Into the depths of the ocean
Or slam me against the life?
Or will it carry me
Above the water
Into the sky
To distant lands
And ancient worlds?

What should I do?
Fight the wind
And stay on the edge
Or let me be carried
At the whim of the wind.
Let the force of destiny
Guide me.
Take me
To the ocean
Or to the sky.

Do I know?
Do I care?
I have reached the edge
Of cliff
Of life
I got there
Now I am here.

Let the force of nature
Decide my next move.

I wait
For the next gust of wind
And let myself
Be at the mercy of the wind.
Wherever it takes me
Is my world
My new world.
My new home.

THE CROSSROADS

I stand
At the crossroads
Of past and the future
Trying to unshackle
The past
To move towards
An uncertain future.

That is me.
That is everyone.

Either we are
Victims of the past
Or creators of the future.

We are one
Yet apart.
We are together
Yet so distant.

We are at the crossroads
Of life
All our life.

THE RAZOR'S EDGE

I stand at the edge
Of the past
And the future
Trying to unshackle
The burdens of the past
To move towards
An uncertain future.

But the present holds me
Chained
To the daily rhythms of life
Moving as undulating waves
As I ride the crest
But staying still.

What to do?

We stand at the edge
The razor's edge
That separates us
The past from the future.

ABOUT MY LIFE

I feel
I grieve
About my life
For what it was
For what it has become.

The change
The destruction
That I inflicted
On my life
The wounds
The scars
And mistakes
Of living
Distort my vision
Of life
And living.

I search for meaning
In an empty shell
I search for purpose
In a vacant heart
A lonely space
In a crowded world.

Everyone is there
But no one is near.
It is all yours
But not yours.

It is life
I feel
I grieve
About my life.

THE STORY OF LIFE

It was a life once
Of happiness
Of future
Of hope of dreams.

Then came a storm
A violent storm
Uprooting trees
Destroying hopes.

And then it was over
A barren land
Devoid of life.
No water
No flowers
An arid land
That needed to bloom again.

There was earth.
There was soil.
There was water.
That's all one needs
For a beginning.

A beginning
Of new hopes
Of new life
Of new world.

A land
That is carved
Out of nothing
Is a land
That is beautiful.

It is you.
You made it.
It is yours
To nurture
And grow
To make it
Into a paradise
Where
Life blooms.

That is
The story of life.

THE ROLLER COASTER

Life is a roller coaster
Ups and downs
At speeds
That you don't control
And never know
When it will end.

It does end
But you don't know
When it ends.

You are at the mercy
Of the designer
Who made the roller coaster
For the designer only knows
How the roller coaster was made.

You are at the whims and moods
of the designer.

The thrills that await you
The ups that soar you
The downs that destroy you
It is the designer
That controls you
Once you step into the ride.

That is life.
It is a roller coaster
Unless you want to take off
And fly off the next curve
To wherever
The momentum takes you.

That is
The roller coaster of life.

THE STORM

It comes
With ferocity
That shakes the earth.

A battle
Between wind and earth
The eternal struggle
Between good and evil
Change and stability
Like life
Which struggles
To maintain
And change.

The storm
Brings force
To shake the foundation
Of existence
Of what is there
And what it
Likes to carve.

Force and power
The energy
That drives civilizations
Sometimes to doom
Is needed
To move ahead
To shake the present
For the future.

It is turbulence
That drives civilizations
To achieve
What it truly is

A place which can survive anything
Or a place
Which comes apart
At the seams.

The storm hits us all
In life
In nature
In world.

It is part of the universe
A part of existence.

Whether one survives
The storm
Depends on what one learns
Resilience
And the ability
To weather the storm
And change.

MY FATHER, MY DAUGHTER

He is dead
My father,
But, he is alive
In my heart
In my spirit
In my veins
And, in my blood.

He gave me
An inquisitive mind
A quest for learning
A gift of life,
And a gift of love.

He taught me
Compassion
Love for fellow kind
To give
But not expect.

How have I done?
Have I lived up to his values?
Maybe not.

But I have a daughter
Who is as lovely
As my father's love was.
She breathes his love
His wisdom
His belief in people
She is him.

I am just a conduit
That facilitates
The passing
Of generations.

Every year
We celebrate
Father's Day
Birthdays
By giving gifts
And having special meals.

What a shame!
When each day
Could be a special day
To count your blessings
And to share
The greatest gift of all
The gift of love and caring.

For it is the only thing
That stays
Forever
Through generations
Just life
My father, my daughter.

ABOUT THE AUTHOR

Dan Khanna considers himself a traveler through life enjoying an adventurous journey.

Dan was born in New Delhi, India. After he completed high school at St. Columbus High School, Dan left India striking out for California via short stays in London, Montreal and Milwaukee, Wisconsin. Although his dream was to pursue a career in the arts, acting, music, and writing, a quirk of fate placed him in engineering college and pursuing a business management career, in which he excelled. Dan completed an undergraduate program in engineering, and a Master and Doctorate in Business Administration.

Dan worked in Silicon Valley's high technology firms and was a CEO and founder of several firms. He changed careers to be a professor. Now, he again is pursuing his dream in creative endeavors.

Dan is the quintessential Renaissance Man, whose interests span the gamut of the arts, sciences, history, social and political studies, classics and philosophy. His search for knowledge began in his early life where his father was the Chief Education Officer of Delhi and his mother was a Sanskrit scholar. Dan speaks English, Hindi, Urdu, Punjabi, and Gujarati.

As a child, Dan read voraciously, particularly enjoying novels, such as Sherlock Holmes, Agatha Christie, Earl Stanley Gardener, Ian Fleming's James Bond series and classic works of Shakespeare, Tolstoy, Dickens, Oscar Wilde, Thomas Hardy, and other writers. He was very interested in poetry and read English poems of Browning, Keats, Milton, Tennyson, and Frost, as well as, other poets, while mastering Urdu poetry. His intellectual interests including studying Western and Eastern philosophers, especially Socrates, from whom he learned questioning methodology employed in his research, lectures and seminars.

During his parochial education, Dan was interested in various sports: cricket, soccer and field hockey. His love for the arts and music was honed to a level that he performed in plays, movies and solo concerts.

Dan's present journey is devoted to creative arts and activities, primarily writing poetry, fiction and non-fiction books and plays, while continuing to acquire knowledge of diverse subjects. He has published one book and has written over twelve hundred poems comprising eighteen books to date. Dan has several non-fiction and fiction books in development.

www.ingramcontent.com/pod-product-compliance
Lightning Source LLC
Chambersburg PA
CBHW071305040426
42444CB00009B/1881